EMILIA IVANCU is a poet, translator and researcher. At present she lives and teaches Romanian language and literature in Poznan, Poland, and holds a position at the University of Alba Iulia, Romania. She has translated Angharad Price's novel *Oh, Tyn y Gorchudd* from Welsh into Romanian as well as the work of Diarmuid Johnson. Her collection of poetry *Jocul de a nu fi mai mult decât sunt/Gra w to, aby nie być więcej niż jestem* was published bilingually in Romanian and Polish (2012) (transl. by Tomasz Klimkowski), and *Şamanii şi poeţii* (2014) is her latest volume of poems, both published by Eikon Publishing House. Her doctoral dissertation is a contribution to the discipline of Postcolonial Studies. Her other publications include *Travels with Steinbeck in Search of America* and *Dictionary of Lucian Blaga's Theatrical Characters* (co-author). In winter, when she writes poetry, she dreams of the Welsh seawaters and the island Enlli, where she believes she will go some day.

DIARMUID JOHNSON was born in Wales and brought up in Ireland. He holds masters and doctoral degrees in Celtic Studies, and has taught and lectured in Ireland, Britain and Europe. He is author and co-author of works of prose and poetry in Welsh, English and Irish, and has translated works from the Welsh of Robin Llywelyn, Aled Islwyn, Dafydd ap Gwilym and Angharad Price into English, Irish, French and Romanian, the latter in collaboration with scholars on the continent. For a number of years, he has been researching the lyric traditions of rural Wales, Romania and other countries.

Washing my Hair with Nettles

Emilia Ivancu

Translated from Romanian with a
postscript by Diarmuid Johnson

Parthian, Cardigan SA43 1ED
www.parthianbooks.com
© Emilia Ivancu 2015
© Translation by Diarmuid Johnson
ISBN 978-1-910409-70-1
Typeset by Elaine Sharples
Printed and bound by Dinefwr Press, Llandybie, Wales
Published with the financial support of the Welsh Books Council.
British Library Cataloguing in Publication Data
A cataloguing record for this book is available from the British Library.

Contents

1

Washing My Hair With Nettles

I picked young nettles while an April moon shone
And while the trees sang cradle-song for the shy grass and
The first lizards bathed in sunlight after a long eclipse.

I picked them, and their needles softly stung my flesh,
And I knew this was the price they had put on the silken water
With which, tomorrow after sunset, I would wash my hair.

Now, into the kettle of simmering water and pungent needles,
I poured, together with the leaves, a flood of dreams
None of which had ever been known to me before.

These are dreams born of nettles, though only once a year,
Dreams seen by eyes that will become mine to see with
Only when silken needles have begun to grow out of my
    waxless hair
Only when fresh nettles have broken through the soil once more
Only when winter has ended, and when the sun has set for the
    last time.

Each Step Reveals a Sign

A sign, each step reveals a sign,
But the senses must remain keen
Lest the moment should pass us by
When the sun's humble rays
Cast a shadow on the cave rock face.
Each step reveals a sign
A reflection in the human eye,
In the woods, hear their dry rustle,
Hear the earth's pulsations.
The palm too, the brow, signs both,
Footsteps, a lock of hair, words you have not spoken.
You shall learn to read them
Only when you have been taught
To shut your eyes
So that night may illuminate your path.
There are signs born with us on our lips,
In death, we hold them in our arms
With signs we shed light on the world
In signs we encrypt the depths of silent wonder.
Do not speak, ripples on the water raise a thousand reflections,
Twofold, fourfold, they multiply
Signs of fear, and sleeping,
Of birth and of death's rigour in the woods.
No man, no stone is without its sign
Signs hum in the smouldering embers
And in speech withheld.
Each step reveals a sign,
The lidden eye, the still lips,
Hands joined on the breast at twilight.
Reading signs from the beyond
We shall know there is no greater beauty
Than when the tall wave
Draws a silent hand
Over a pool of burning sunset.

In Every Garden

In every garden there ever was in Eden a serpent still remains
Just as between the pages of each book there lurks a demon.
And when the serpent raises slow its tail
And the demon blinks a still eye
From the branch a hundred apples thunder to the ground
And through the words there runs a tremor.
Childlike, innocent, the people hasten to gather word and fruit
Hungry to taste of life together with its boundless yearning.
As they sink their teeth into the sun-red apple,
The golden juices, burning with promise, run across their lips
As though from wax-coloured pages
But now their hands are shot through with darting pain
And they sense the heart cloud within them.

In every garden there ever was in Eden a serpent still remains
Just as between the pages of every book there lurks a demon.
And the demon stalks us, poised to strike,
Fangs bared to sting our flesh,
And how eagerly we eat both word and apple
While all the time, in sky and earth, our breath is dissipated.

Sleep

I dreamt I had lain down by the seashore on a rock to sleep,
To put my dreams to sleep, to suspend the spinning wheels of
   life.
The shadow of a wave clothed me
Into depths I descended where no fish will go
For fear they might swallow their own scales.
Into the depths I dived that my tired eyes might sleep
To recall what I once had been before I was born.

Feeling my way through the dark
Searching for traces of those who inhabited the world before me
Of those destined to be born when my time is past.

I dreamt that I was diving into jade-clear waters
To send to sleep the unlived dreams
To send to sleep the forgotten songs
To find again the eyes, once mine, that I had lost,
Eyes mine on that day when first I saw the light.

I dreamt I had lain down by the seashore on a rock
To sleep, to put my dreams to sleep, to suspend the spinning
   wheels of life.

Never Tell a Blind Man He Is Blind

Never tell a blind man he is blind
His eyes though open wide see only the world within.
The many hands swimming in his boundless ocean
Shall never be revealed to him.
His eyes shall only perceive
How the dark wrests from them the light they have never
    known.
Never tell a blind man he is blind
Better simply to offer him the gift of three water-blossoms
And a fistful of earth.

Shamans and Poets

There are things only poets and shamans can say
Only they, because death, real or imagined,
The fears, the terror-filled silences of others
These they know how to steal
And carry across the border to another world
A place where there is neither death nor pain
A place others too might wish to go
Though fear retains them, fear of pain, fear of death.
Each incantation, each invocation,
Achieves no less than to show the world
That any man, should he refuse to kill,
Can vanquish death.
Each refusal to kill
Renews the breath that moves across the earth
Reviving its very charm, reviving too its dreams.
Poets when possessed with the urge to kill
Soon find a way to steal the silences, the shattered dreams
And quickly cross the border
Giving birth to a new world
Restoring to the old its charm,
Bringing new dreams fresh, clad in green.
Refusal to kill shall overcome death no matter when,
Refusal to kill, whether man, beast, flower or dream,
This is why there are things that only shamans and poets can
    say
Only they can reach this place which knows neither death nor
    pain
Carrying an armful of broken dreams and terror-filled silences
Gathered together inside them
And should fortune favour them
These dreams, with closed eyes and deepening breath,
They shall inscribe on a leaf of paper.

Two Questions

When the last storm of winter had broken over us
Turning the tears to ice upon our cheeks
I asked myself
How much a man can lose in the space of a single day.
Much, little, the answer is not simple,
But what do these two words imply?
In the iron-depths of winter
There can be no doubt: a man risks all.
And once another claimed that
When a good man suffers
It enhances the kindness of his heart.
Seeing the narcissus flower, knowing love wide as the sea
The world and its charm are recharged to the core.
We drank of suffering though it was not a poison cup
Rather a jug of young wine, juice of grape fermenting.
They watched us, they cursed us, causing all things to perish,
But the daylight world rose again out of a turquoise sea,
Turquoise sea where, in a single drop of salt dew, carried by the
    last storm of winter,
The seed of the narcissus flower had dropped from a cloud.
What can a man recover in the space of a single day?
The question pales before its answer.
In the space of a day a man can recover
As much as the love that he could give.

Stones on the Seashore

On the seashore, there is beauty in the stones
On sun-rich days when you might take one
And place it on a throbbing shoulder.

But if raised up and hurled to strike the bone,
Though the sun be bright
This shoulder will suffer pain greater than it has ever felt.

And in the stone there is latent proof,
As in every book and stone there ever was,
That where-ever a stone may lie
There lie two forces, side by side,
One to heal, the other to destroy.

And so too we, side by side,
So too suffering and bliss
Wrestling naked on the warm bed.

Man Is a Boat

The flaw is inherent, man will err,
Who then shall place a stone on the grave of the voice that told
    the tale?
Under this sky, and under no other, a thousand waves will
    break.
Into this sea, and into no other, a thousand gulls will dive.

From this hot and sunburnt shore, each of us steals one stone
Steals the corner-stone of the tide
Forgetting that man too is as a boat
Rocking gently in the swell
Where the four winds converge.

But who will dare hold the hand that carried the stone away?
Who will return to the shore all the stones ever taken since
The first wave broke over the rock
In its fury to reach the edges of the moon?

Man too, man is a boat,
Rocking gently between past errors and others soon to be
    committed
So that each day, as he re-enacts the tale,
Recalling the unending labour of Sisyphus of old,
He will return to the grey shore
All stones ever stolen since time first began.

Medusa Dies

They say the medusa swim their way toward the island
Seeking death there upon its shores.
They too, chainless in the cold ocean blue,
Set out on their final journey
To the world's end
Where water shall always be rather
The place where the road begins.
Washed up from a world of waves that the eye can see
The medusa choose death,
Rejoicing for the first and last time
In the hot sun's fatal embrace.

I Am a Garden With but a Single Tree

I am a garden with but a single tree
But this tree of mine, it is a forest.
Under its branches, there is rest for fieldfuls of white
    snowdrops.
Mornings in which I raise my arms to the sky
These I love
Mornings flowing with milky light
Mornings when birds awake in their star-shaped nests
Mornings, warm or cool,
When the sky is so close
That somehow I feel dizzy.
I am a garden with but a single tree
But this tree of mine, it is a forest
And in my arms, clouds sit a while to rest,
And, roofed only by the sky, both the living and the dead
    continue on their road.

Wafting through my leaves, the aroma of their fresh coffee
Calls to mind
Those who sleep beneath the waters,
Faces buried in the woods and lost in time,
A spear hurled through the dragon's heart,
In the rushes, the spirit of the lake.

Under the tree, people meet to grind the black beans,
To spin these tales that shall never be forgotten.
I am a garden with a single tree
But this tree of mine, it is a forest.

Walking on Water

I have longed so much to walk on water
And have wished to feel the sea tongue my toes,
To have fish come, and together with me on my journey,
Swim their way out into the ocean.
So much I have longed to touch the sky with both temples
So often dreamt that my brow was melting in the sunlight
My mind rising like a column.
So much I wished to wrap myself in bandages of ice
And feel the cold shiver within me
Until all non-being should fall away
From shoulders, thighs and breasts.
I have longed so much
And now I shudder
More than cold could ever make me do
And where once there were shoulders, thighs and breasts
Algae have grown upon me, long green algae,
Who long so much, long so much
To walk with me on water.

The Cup

I have placed within me
In the body's empty core
A cup of living water,
Moon-round, edges jagged as the knife
With which I cut bread
To leave for you each morning
On the threshold.
The cup sustains in me
The cycle of dreams and madness,
A cup of living water
From which the birds will drink
Each year come autumn
Before they undertake their longest flight.
A cup of living water
Which, drop by drop, should it all evaporate,
You in turn might fill
And with your body.

The Air Is All I Have

I have nothing -
No place to weep,
No place in which to die.
Times are I do find a corner of this world in which to sleep
But it's never more than somewhere rented.
I can look into the hearts and homes of others
But always only through the window;
All doors are meant for those who live within.
After a time
Even when drinking tea with friends
There comes a moment when I must leave -
I don't even trouble to say that I would like to stay
And once again I peer through the window
Smiling, though in no way embittered,
At the thought that I too could have people come to tea or
    coffee.
I have nothing -
This is why I do not wish to give myself up to the earth -
Being rootless, I have reason not to.
So you may let the wind carry me away
The air is all I have
I feel it, breathe it, but never can I touch it.

II

Andrey Rublow

Over a grey hill
Decked with small white flowers
Dark horses ran
In joy.

The icon painter
Passing the poplar trees by the roadside
Thought to paint the world all in colour.

The monastery walls Manole had built
They were still blank and silent
Until...

In a single brush-stroke
Beginning with a point in space
The world burst into colour

And assumed the form of a chalice.

Over a verdant hill
Decked with small flowers red, yellow, red, yellow, blue
Bay horses ran
In joy.

The icon painter
Passing the poplar trees by the roadside
Thought to pause and rest a while
And so he sat in the chalice.

The monastery walls Manole had built
Were all in colour now and so they sang

And the monastery was a chalice
In which they slept
both Manole and the icon painter.

St John's Night

In the idiom of Romanian folk tradition

By the church door she stood, and there she waited for me,
Her wiry hair buttered up with snakes made of cream
In her right hand, a sprig she held, of basil so green
Tied up with a hair from the tail of a rollicking steed.

With her left hand she gestured, and I stepped promptly inside
And her black-toothed smile was a cue for the birds of the night
When I went in, there was John, painted in prayer icons bright,
I wished that the priest might bless me, my fate and my plight.

But the priest danced a dance round the altar, heel toe heel toe,
And on both his shoulders two pigeons sit perched as he goes
In the church there was no-one, to the roof no singing voice
    rose
The priest still danced on in a silence that beautifully glowed.

And so out I went, hand in hand with a crow,
Come down from a sky painted by Andrey Rublow
Sat on a web spun by a spider so slow
But the witch she had left, and now I was standing alone.

The night all around had grown most eerie and blind
I could feel the crow leading me on, he held my hand tight,
And there it was plain, a miracle born of the night,
The stone had been moved, but who could have pushed it
    aside?

Flute-Player Returns

He walked backwards as he came
Preferred not to run, took measured steps,
And counted the stones on his path to guide him.
The symmetry of his movements seemed to please him:
No step greater, no step lesser than
A stumbling thought on the uneven way.
As he walked he played on the shadowy flute
And when women heard him
They shut their windows tight
Hurrying to cover their children's ears.
When young maids heard him,
They undid their plaited hair, and ran with abandon across the
    hills
Singing with moon and sun.
When the young men heard him
They prayed to heaven
For strength to follow.
The horse and ox, unchained,
Began to dance in circles
Telling old wives' tales to the wise.
Flowers turned to buds
And green branches sprouted on the roofs.
The flute-man walked ever further
The world ahead grew and grew
The world behind became ever rounder
And now the music faded to an echo,
The flute began to turn into a cherry tree
And slowly, slowly the man was swallowed by the earth.

Mistmaids at Midsummer

They are dancing, they are spinning, they are luscious in the
  moonlight
And their singing fills the valleys and they sing about the
  willow
And running now you see them, and running you will lose them
And now your eyes are burning, there are hands upon the
  willow
And their locks might brush your cheeks as their shadows
  disappear
And their singing is of weeping and the singing it is booming
And their dancing makes you sleepy, and their dancing draws
  you nearer
And the wind is theirs to straddle, and running you are running
And now your head is spinning and you are lost and fading
They are dancing, they are spinning, they are luscious in the
  moonlight
And their singing fills the valleys and they sing about the
  willow
And their singing fills the valleys and they sing about the
  willow
And they sing about the willow
And they sing about the willow.

She Is

Falling hair veils her eyes
But she can see the sky.

The waves conceal her thighs
But she is there, swimming, swimming.

Behind the leaves, there are hidden flowers
With time, they will bear their fruit.

And though silence may rob her of her speech
Listen, listen, maybe you shall hear her.

Yes, she is there:
A rustle in the twilight.

April Snow

Only the mind hastens over late April snow
Young snow falling and settling, falling and settling
But growing heavier on the shoulders of the world.
The eye sweeps disoriented across the open ground
Knowing the earth here once reached for the sky with green
    fingers.
Racing through the empty silence
As if gripped by a claw
My gaze settles
On a herd of deer in the vast and burning snow;
Driven by hunger, they have set out
To beg for their food at bright windows in the village.
As night draws near, snowfall thickening,
Hunger too deepens in the gut,
Driving all things to the limit of their ken.

But in the clouds a distant movement attracts the eye –
The storks, returning from warmer climes!
They wonder now what unknown hand has blessed the world
That, as the day dies,
The deer abandon caution
And leave their wood to sing a child to sleep
Whose face a window frames.

Carrying the Sky on Our Shoulders

Today the sky has climbed down from above
The clouds are sinking weightlessly.
The rain is keeping off, but now,
After a summer when the sky carried all the blazing world in its
    arms
The time has come for it to rest its heavy though unleaden
    wings.
And so it settles upon our shoulders
To rest for one short day.

Time of late has been draining into us
Just as leaves in autumn swirl in a sleeve of wind,
Falling in droves, all in disarray, and whispering underfoot.
And as they sweep around us,
We the heedless look beyond them
Into the fresh green of other springs to come.
In this way, as autumn grows, we hear a voice say
That, just as leaves do,
Other things we claim to know
May hide their own unknown colours.

Today the sky has climbed down from above
But weighs little on our willing shoulders
And all things yearn to rest their soul—
Tree and bird, the grass, we too
On whom today the tired sky has fallen
After the racing joy of summer.
But, come tomorrow when it rises,
We shall straighten our bent limbs
And claim our load was greater
Than ever weighed on the tall sky.

Today the sky has climbed down from above
But shed no tears! Let us be glad,
And embrace this day as we would a reddened leaf.
And come tomorrow when the sky has risen,
Branching arms and arm-like branches
Shall give voice to words that bind us to other things unseen,
Thin threads of burden, a hundred shades rich, woven through
   sky and bone.

Shadowtide

There shall be no word spoken today
Only the humming song we breathe.
The eyelid floats gently
Light swirls inward and expires.
In the void, see a pall of smoke rise:
The days have burned their last
And turned to ash
It is time for us to hide our eyes in the last glow of an
    ember
And feel the great dark exhale
Its jaws gaping monstrous.
Night grows to oust the ailing day
As though the moon were bearing an eclipse.
From afar, through the black, echoes come,
Words whispered, song passing into another orbit.
Then silence falls.
The earth dies in the jaws of winter
The sun lies cold on its bier
The acrid smell of hot ash prevails.
There shall be no word spoken today
Until the bells ring faintly and a branch of sun
Reddens a cheek of wooden earth,
Its fire slowly spreading to our hands
And to the fingers of the singing ivy.
The root stirs in its deep bed
And the people say:
"We are blessed, an infant sun is born."

III

Enlli

I

A book, a map, and silence;
With these you begin your journey to the island of the saints.
Their names are to be found in no almanac, neither on the altar,
But their words breathe deep beneath the sea.

Should you wish to turn for home,
Unlike the page that you now read
whose letters remain unchanged tomorrow,
The road that unwinds before you
may not be open when you return

And words you choose not to utter
will bloom again on every tree along the way
While things spoken yesterday
will by then long since have expired.

All that you may wish to find in others
you will find, but only in yourself,
All you may have given to the world
will sleep tomorrow with shadows and the sea.

When things come, they come to us in silence,
should we choose to call them in song and dream.
If chained down, they will resist
and strive to destroy all words made of thunder, lightning or
    fire.

Sing to things that they may come to you,
sing to them of pilgrims and blue springs,
of sea blue green, silent and shifting,

31

of the holy mountain
that will not weep in autumn when the birds leave.
Sing to them of saints who sleep deep in the waters,
Then perhaps the road which unwinds before you
will be open if you should return.

Of all things you may consider sacred
that you encounter along your mortal way,
You will choose perhaps those whose colours change like the
    surface of the sea,
and return in spring as do the birds,
always in a swirling flock, though others of their kind.

II

Whitened by the salt, the bones became a bridge,
dried by the winter sun, the veins are ropes
to help us cross the border into another realm
while our bodies, together with their shadows, remain behind.

From the deep, hands beckon to us,
and for our sake other eyes strain to penetrate the dark.
Sunken bones draw a ripple from the coursing waters
and longings, many longings wash across the shore.

Over the bridge of salt-white bone
we throw trawls of stony prayer
and let them sink to the black depths
amongst the algae and seals with weepy eyes.

The bridge of saintly bone sways on the wave,
as, silently, and to ourselves,
we utter a thousand shapeless words,
a thousand meanings held in book and breast
to cross the border and return
whiter than the bridge of bone.

The seals splash and tumble on the shore
their slow eyes brushing the horizon.
From one dawn to the next a century has passed.
In the searing sunlight,
the white bones are lost to the eye,
Now words and their thousand meanings
have melted between two shores,
one snow-cheeked, the other cradled in the sea.

Sky and earth, we crossed them both,
returning to ourselves, as the hermit to its crab-shell.
Slowly and in silence we returned, like the changing waters of
the sea,
and like the mountains, looming behind their curtain of mist.

In this corner of the world where the bridge of bones remains a
dream
the white shell was placed upon the shore
and in it may still be heard
the roaring waters and their distant yearning.

III

Though we had travelled far, now we stood at the centre of the
　　world.
With book and map we had set out
seeking the place where all things once a burden now seem
　　feather-light,
and where the salmon sleeps
eyes wide open to the moon.
Valley, mountain, mountain, valley,
and birds screaming of distance
where people's eyes are full of silence.
The earth spun with us
and the sea spun inside us like a crystal globe.
All that lies ahead soon shall be behind us
but none of what we left behind
shall ever reappear before us.
The road that once unwound before us
is never the one to bring us home.
During the journey trees have bloomed,
and returning we eat the ripened apples.
The birds circled above as many days flew by.
In my right hand a map, book in my left,
they have restored colour to the world.
The whale-island was breathing blue and green
as together we inhaled the salty sky.
Now the returning road
becomes the path where first we trod
though neither of them knows the other.
The salmon sleeps eyes wide open
dreaming with us of a crystal globe,
in which the sea spins a whale-island.

To Forget Jerusalem

Jerusalem, Jerusalem!
I shall come and lay my head on your sand and stones
I shall come to drink of your cold indifference
I shall come that you might forget all that has ever been
That you might come to know who in truth you are.

Until now I have slept in caves
Bathing as I did in darkened waters
Next to my skin I have worn a shirt of coarse hair
Neither cheese nor meat I have eaten
No wine has passed my lips.

Screaming I told them that mine too was flesh bruised and
    black
And, tearing my hair by the root, I raised the sea to a storm
Then, removing my shoes, I continued barefoot through the
    world,
Burying my face now in such ashes as I found.

Nobody heard me, Jerusalem,
I too bore wounds but they remained unseen
None combed my hair
Nor gave me wine to drink
And each time that I died
No-one came to have me buried.

I have come to ask that you forget it all
I have come to ask you for a piece of wood, an apple
I come arms laden with wine
Milk oozing from my breasts
Though empty-wombed.

Jerusalem, Jesusalem
Accept these all my gifts
Accept them, then hurl them into the sea,
Make the sea rise and engulf me
Give me water to drink
Give me life that I might die
And when you have forgotten all
You shall come to know who in truth you are.

Two Women of Armenia

I dreamed that you wrote me a poem:
In it they appeared, two women of Armenia,
They moved in convoy with other bluish shapes
Whose hair, midnight-black, falling to the waist,
The desert had taken from them,
Bluish shapes whose eerie shadows had remained
Under a burning desert sky to watch over their milkless young,
Their milkless young, their menfolk, ravaged by the winds
With never a hand to bury them.
To me you wrote of their roofless weeping
Like waves heaving in a storm that will not abate.
So too of Ararat you wrote to me
Where the white vultures fly alone
While others, black, have been struck down,
Cursed by the earth
When they stained hill and valley in carrion blood
Young as the morning dew.
You wrote to me of the scars concealed in people's smiling
Who refuse hate a licence to consume them,
And how, in a single lifetime, time and again, we may succumb
    to death
Yet, despite our dying, we sentence no-one to the grave,
For this concerns no other than God and us.
You wrote to say you would send the gods to raise me up
If, bound for the peak of Ararat, I should ever fall,
To say how the white vultures would heal of their wounds my
    knees, my arms.
And then when I awoke I no longer was myself
But a shadow, moving on the desert, among the women of
    Armenia,
Those whose wounds none had nursed
Those whose children none had fed with milk,

Those whose menfolk none had buried.
And since that time my waiting has never ceased,
Waiting for a sign given by those gods that you invoke
Waiting for a glimpse of white vultures on the wing.

The Trees Have Numbers in This Town

The trees have numbers in this town
And the streets here play hide-and-seek.
You think of the hand that pens the word and feel yourself
    shudder with delight.
In this town, things have a different feel,
They are not born in the heart
As was believed for centuries,
But in the mind, in the stomach.
Only in this town where tree number 28
Says 'Guten Tag' each day
Can you come to know the secret
Of how to withstand gusting wind and rain
Even if you have no roots.
Only here, where light and shadow play their game,
Can you find candles on the breakfast table
And birds, flying in through your open window, to make you
    smile.
Only here, where each tree has a number,
Will the train door open at the very place where a friend stands
    on the platform.
Only in this, the town of the numbered trees,
Can you hope to see the mirror smile back at you
No matter where you choose a place to hide.
But here, to the town where trees have numbers,
You can return at any time
And hope that you too may grow roots and leaves
And that birds will always fly here off the tongue.

The Bridge

Long nights and days I walked across the desert
Carrying with me a full sack, heavy, not as a stone,
But as a duck swimming on a lake.
I walked the paths of the wise mages
Following the sounds of music flowing from the light.
Soon, in the silence of the desert,
Where the light transforms and liberates the mind,
I reached the river.
The river sang there like a swan
And its song became a bridge
Crossing the face of the water but crossing it below the surface
    too.
And whilst offering to take me to the other bank
The bridge kept these two worlds from inching closer.
Bridge in heart now
I turned, and set out for home.

IV

Harmony

Listening to guitar and flute music in Râmeţi, Romania

Tremor of string, hum of wood
The wind wipes a wet cheek
And hands the sky its scarf.
Now dew glistens on thatched roofs
And the eye flickers faintly
As, in the well, the waters suspend their flow.
Tremor of string, hum of wood:
We listen to the mountain dreaming.

Seven Years

For this time on until seven years have passed
I shall begin and end each day
Eyes raised to the mountain that my window overlooks
The better always to remember
That a man comes into this world
That the mountain
And not he
May climb
Climb into the sky.

The Game of Being No More Than
I Really Am

See how the bird flies,
see how all that I dream at night takes shape come day
see how my silence deepens
so that each word uttered may reinforce the world.

See how when the world trembles
and with it I too tremble
guilty of a moment's happiness while the walls crumble.

See how every spring I wait for the snowdrops to emerge
in order to convince myself
that only man is mortal
and still
see how, not for a single moment, can I imagine the world
    without me,
nor understand how man, stained with sin, now hosts death,
but is revered as master of the world.

See how every day I see them,
shoulders stooping, cumbersome headphones in place,
people who, as each day passes,
wish to isolate themselves more and more in an illusion of
    peace.
see how every day I play ever more earnestly
the game of being no more than I really am.

Geranium

The red geranium I bought this morning
Smiles now
A gaping wound by the window.
And so, when they pass my door, the tall people choose to look
  away
But the little ones, sweetly complicit,
They smile and pause to look
Because they know the geranium red has come from faraway
From a land where all colour has its source,
All joy, all the cuts and grazes of this life.

Left Hand

One day a man gave me a book
and said his entire life was written there.
Leafing through its pages,
I felt the letters vivid
under my damp frozen hand and darkened eyes.
The pages spoke of yellow, and blue and black,
and smelt of freshly mown grass
mingled with ink.
While I was reading, the colours were mirrored in my eyes
and there were faces swimming there,
and breakfast mornings at the bar around the corner,
and many, many icons
all written with the left hand.

Feathers at Dawn

Each day when we meet
Without touching a single feather
You place a bird in the palm of my hand
And show me how, while on the wing,
It never doubts the reason for its flight
Nor questions where it may be bound.
Returning each day, you perch on my shoulder,
Silent as a river, a murmur among fish and stones.
Each time we meet
I remember how, for an instant,
The passing hour swallows itself up
And how we find respite
In those quiet waters.
Each day I pick feathers from the path
- A hushed sign you leave for me -
Lest I should think you too had been consumed by time.
Feathers so that, come morning,
From my window I may see once more
A flock of birds in flight.

Siberian Winter

The Siberian winter has come,
Words have frozen on my lips,
like stones, hard and big,
like lumps of rock.
A burden, a sharp pain,
they lie heavy
in my mouth and body,
dragging me down to earth.
Words have frozen on my lips,
and now the only cry is silence.

Swallows

When I was a child, I watched the swallows come in spring
They nested in the terrace of our apple-scented house.
And I, wishing only to fly,
Would gather the feathers they shed,
Wings in autumn outbound for other waters.

Years passed,
The house clothed itself in shadow,
Nests fell empty
No swallows returned there
Nor did I.

Now, twenty summers on,
I house a burning candle,
And the swallows are returning.

Just as long ago,
I gathered up the feathers
Feathers that tell me of their autumn journey,
Hoping that, come spring,
While the candle burns within me,
The swallows will cross an ocean and find the flame.

The World Is but an Endless Sea of Mist

The world is but an endless sea of mist
And through the world I went
My eyes those of fox, of forest and of wave,
Those too of all who ever went before me
Before I then became none other than myself
Before, with eyes of my own, I saw the light.

The first half of my life, this I spent reading books,
Some long and some concise,
Sweeping down a mountainside, a slope of dream,
My skis the insights that remain
When all is read, read and then forgotten.

The next part of my life I spent a pilgrim
Between Mount Eremos and the Mount of Olives
In the grip of sudden storm, a gift to me from the world,
And, living on nothing but olives,
Savouring their slow bliss, always mine,
Never thinking to feed off that of others,
In this way I survived.

I no longer know where I am today
Nor with whose eyes I see
Though these things carry no importance.

Today, in this the third half of my life,
I delight in all sweet tastes one can find
High on the slope, or deep in the mountain's shadow,
And if patience should suffice
To forget all things one can read in a lifetime
Hand on heart, I can say no more that this;
The world is but an endless sea of mist.

Postscript

A World of Myth and Symbols

The poetry of Emilia Ivancu invites us to discover a culture largely unknown to readers of western literature. Here, in the greater Danube basin, a world of myth and symbolism remains intact. And while history will tell us that the open plains and remote mountains of the Balkans were the stage on which the Ottoman and Austro-Hungarian empires fought, in the literatures of the region we find other mysteries, and the thread of narratives that reach back not centuries but millenia.

In Romania, we find rich expression of these things, fed by a classical past, Latin and Greek, by sustained exchanges over time with German and French culture, and by its own traditions which lend the modern Romanian lyric its character, its unique voice and its many colours. Here, rupture between the medieval and modern epochs is of no major significance. The orthodox world retains much of its early resonance. It has not undergone the fragmentation that causes the *malaise* of the west.

In the author's note to her second collection, *Shamans and Poets,* Emilia Ivancu writes as follows: 'Poetry expresses the inexpressible, the intangible, things that happen between two breaths, the shape the eye takes while closing, while opening. Poetry expresses wordlessness.' The poem *Shamans and Poets* tells us more of Emilia Ivancu's vision of the poet and his or her calling: 'He finds a way to steal the broken dreams, giving birth to a new world'.

Exploring the idea of wordlessness, we soon find ourselves in the visual world, and in this case, that of Andrey Rublow, the Russican icon-painter from the 13th century. In the work of Rublow, shape was given to things that had existed only in word before, and to the shape Rublow added colour, thus giving new meanings to old things. Icons, Rublow says, are windows.

When opening *Washing My Hair With Nettles,* and looking through the window, what things do we see? A leading literary critic, Daniel Cristea-Enache, recently spoke as follows of the work of Emilia Ivancu: 'She swims against the mainstream of Romanian poetry. But she swims upstream, coming closer to the sources of ancient symbols. And swimming in deep waters, her work brings to the surface things that have lain dormant for long periods of time'.

These things include the one tree that is a forest. The shaman and the poet. The medusa dying in the sun's fatal embrace. We see the world in *Sleep* through the eye of a fox. In *Two Women of Armenia*, we see Mount Ararat, witness to genocide in 1915. We see Jerusalem, mistmaids at midsummer. We see Bardsey Island (Welsh 'Enlli') through the eyes of a pilgrim, and signs that are revealed with every step. How do we learn to read these signs? To do so we must enter the Balkan world.

II

The great cathedrals of England, France and Germany epitomise a view of the world as held by the medieval Christian mind in Western Europe. These edifices reach out to the sky in longing. They cast huge shadows and humble the beholder. Their message is clear: feet rooted to the earth, man is a lesser being than all the things celestial and high. Such cathedrals do not exist in Romania. Here, as elsewhere in the Balkans and the orthodox world, there are other models; the low-roofed monastery, for example, a place where the faithful wait with dignity for divine grace to descend amongst them. In *Carrying the Sky on Our Shoulders*, we read: 'Today the sky has climbed down from above, but weighs little on our willing shoulders, and all things yearn to rest their soul…'

Inhabiting the margins of the human world in Balkan culture, and in the poetry of Emilia Ivancu, we find shapes and shadows, figments of the subconscious perhaps, not spirits as such but simply other beings. These are not always hostile to their mortal neighbours, but seem to represent some danger, at least to the innocent. Amongst these we find *Ielele*, the *Mistmaids at Midsummer*: 'They are dancing, they are spinning, they are luscious in the moonshine, and their singing fills the valleys and they sing about the willow'.

In the poem *St John's Night,* we encounter another nameless, otherworldly female figure whose presence is indicative of the chaos that reigns when the daylight hours have reached their ultimate span. The poet writes: 'By the church door she stood, and there she waited for me, her wiry hair buttered up with snakes made of cream, in her right hand, a sprig she held, of basil so green, tied up with a hair from the tail of a rollicking steed'.

Other poems too in this collection are inspired by a culture of folk religion. In *Shadowtide*, a poem for mid-winter, we read: 'The days have burned their last and turned to ash, it is time for us to hide our eyes in the last glow of an ember, and feel the great dark exhale, its jaws gaping monstrous'. Here the metaphor for mid-winter stops short of personification, but we clearly see the figurative imagination at work.

In the poem *She Is*, the personification of a perceived presence in the world is developed from the folk vein by the poet into a verbal equivalent of an impressionistic painting. We read: 'Though silence may steal her speech, listen, listen, you shall hear her. She is there: 'A rustle in the twilight'.

In the poetry of Emilia Ivancu, we find women who wash their hair with nettles, carry the world on their shoulders, walk on water, women who say that the air is all they have. The woman suffers, but her world is not colonised by the male world. She is free, free but human. She has the power given to her by earth and sea, though this power is also hers to lose.

Within Byzantian tradition therefore, we see what might be referred to as 'pagan' beliefs and customs continuing to form part of the culture of the people, a culture fully accepted by the church, and interwoven together with it, despite the monotheism that Christianity purports to advocate.

III

In Western culture, aesthetics play an important part in the appreciation of art. The domination of the common man by the greater powers above, and the sentiments that this induces, made of art a refuge where, if only transitorially, beauty and respite could be found from a more cruel world. Western art makes of aesthetic beauty an objective and a goal in its own right. In parts of the East, this does not apply in the same way. What *does* apply? We find the answer in mythology.

The mythological space is still vibrant in Romania today, and contrasts with the largely post-mythological space of Western Europe and Britain. To live in the mythological space is to be part of a world animated by symbols and tradition, and to share with other forms of life, fauna and flora, an environment built from earth, sky, mountain and time. But time here is not linear, not a hostile force that exhausts human life. Time is cyclical, and being cyclical is benign. Emanating from within this mythological space, the poetry of Emilia Ivancu is an expression of the things human culture was built on during the centuries and millenia that precede the mechanisation and industrialisation that characterises the present era. This mechanisation and industrialisation is one of the catalysts in the demythologisation of the modern world. The reason for this is a question of animacy.

In the older animate world, all things were an expression of the intrinsic vitality of a world that constantly renewed itself, a process man too was part of, and a thing he celebrated with rite and ritual. Mechanisation and industrialisation changes this state of affairs fundamentally. The natural rhythms of growth, decay and rebirth are replaced with ideas of acceleration and progress. The natural balance that enables the world to renew its vitality is challenged and overwhelmed by ideas of exploitation and productivity.

In this way, the mythological space becomes a post-mythological one. The latent meaning of things is replaced by a material value assigned to them. And the latent significance of objects that occur in the world is replaced by the idea of an aesthetic value attributed to them. Latency of meaning and significance in the mythological space is replaced in this way by the blatancy of material and aesthetic value in the post-mythological space. The poetry of Emilia Ivancu is an expression of the former.

The notion of latency lies at the heart of the work in other ways too. In *Stones on the Seashore* we read: 'Where-ever a stone may lie, there lie two forces, side by side, one to heal, the other to destroy'. And in *Carrying the Sky on Our Shoulders*: 'In this way, as autumn grows, we hear a voice say that, just as leaves do, other things we claim to know may hide their own unknown colours'.

Here the poet is expressing a view that uses some of the vocabulary of dualism, a view however that is distinct from dualism in that it admits none of the polarisation of the benign and the malign that occurs in dualistic systems of thinking. The poet believes that the benign and the malign are latent in all things, but form the essence of none.

In Europe, the rural space is the cradle of the culture of mythology, and the gradual discontinuation of traditional human culture in the rural space in modern Europe, together with the resultant urbanisation that had begun by the nineteenth century, has led to an alienation of the modern mind from the place where its understanding of the world began. Isolated by this alienation, the poet stands alone in the world. Thus in *Siberian Winter* we read: 'Words have frozen on my lips, and then the only cry is silence'. And in *Jerusalem*: 'Nobody heard me, Jerusalem, none combed my hair nor gave me wine to drink, and each time I died, no-one came to have me buried'.

The notion of isolation leads us to consider the individual space, markedly different in the traditional and modern worlds respectively. Survival in isolation has been made possible by mechanisation, and in western society this isolation is cultivated and valued. In the traditional space, on the other hand, individuality is far less sustainable. Emilia Ivancu's *The Game of Being No More Than I Really Am,* a poem that gives her first collection its title, is informed by the tensions that arise from the individualisation of space, and from the isolation and freedom that occur in tandem due to this individualisation. She writes: 'Every day I see them, shoulders stooping, cumbersome headphones in place, people who, as each day passes, wish to isolate themselves more and more'.

Coming to the urban from the rural space, and from a world where the latent meaning of things remains strong, the city as seen through the eyes of the poet undergoes a process of reanimation, and is, though briefly perhaps, recolonised by the symbol-making mind. In *The Trees Have Numbers in This Town,* a playful poem of child-like innocence, we read: 'Only here, where light and shadow play their game, can you find candles on the breakfast table, and birds, flying in through your open window, to make you smile. Only here, where each tree has a number, will the train door open at the very place where a friend stands on the platform...'

The name 'Manole' occurs in the poem *Andrey Rublow*. We read: 'The monastery walls Manole had built, they were still blank and silent until, in a single brush-stroke beginning with a point in space, the world burst into colour'. Manole is a master-builder in Romanian mythology and built the monastery at Curtea de Argeş in Southern Romania. He gives his name to a ballad, widespread in oral tradition, in which, to ensure his edifice will remain solid with the passage of time, he is said to make a human sacrifice: he has his wife walled into the stone structure of the monastery.

The reference to Manole in the poetry of Emilia Ivancu illustrates several things that are crucial to a reading of her work and to an understanding of Romanian and Balkan culture and literature. First, tradition there is ancient, but vibrant, and its symbols are real and poignant. Second, the oral tradition remains a vehicle for this tradition, and the distinction between written and oral, popular and intellectual is by no means clear-cut or complete. In fact, just as in Celtic tradition, Welsh or Gaelic, one enhances the other. Third, the idea of the sacrifice expressed in the Manole myth, is relevant to the underlying philosophy expressed in the poetry of Emilia Ivancu. This is a philosophy of the symbol. According to this philosophy, nothing in the world is without a meaning waiting to be revealed. The poem *Each Step Reveals a Sign*, one of several *ars poetica* in this collection, expresses as well as any the tenants of this philosophy: 'Each step reveals a sign, footsteps, a lock of hair, words you have not spoken. You shall learn to read them only when you have been taught to shut your eyes so that night may illuminate your path'.

D.J. 2014

Acknowledgement

We would like to thank Valentin Ajder (Eikon Publishing House, Romania) for the copyright of the texts, as well as his support.

Note

Emilia Ivancu (Romania) and Diarmuid Johnson (Wales), together with Tomasz Klimkowski (Poland) are co-founders of ARADOS (2009), a Society for the appreciation of poetry and lyric traditions in the Celtic, Romanian, and Polish languages.

www.aradospoetry.org

PARTHIAN

Washing My Hair With Nettles

Emilia Ivancu

Tattoo on Crow Street

Kate Noakes

Living in the
Delta

new & collected poems

Landeg White

Book of
songs

Herman Schmenk

POETRY